Hop-Skip-Jump-a-roo Zoo

by Jane Belk Moncure
illustrated by Linda Hohag
and Dan Spoden

Published by

Mankato, Minnesota

The Library —
A Magic Castle

Come to the magic castle
When you are growing tall.
Rows upon rows of Word Windows
Line every single wall.
They reach up high,
As high as the sky,
And you want to open them all.
For every time you open one,
A new adventure has begun.

Andy opens a Word Window.
Guess what he sees?

A zoo gate.

The zoo gate is open wide, so Andy skips inside.

He sees one elephant in the zoo.
What can one elephant do?

He can swing and sway his trunk this way.

Andy can do that too.
Can you?

Andy sees two giraffes in the zoo. What can two giraffes do?

They can stretch their necks high as Andy walks by.

Andy can do that too.
Can you?

Andy sees three polar bears in the zoo.
What can three polar bears do?

They can swim in a pool so they will
keep cool.

Andy can do that too.
Can you?

Andy sees four camels in the zoo.
What can four camels do?

They can carry packs upon their backs.

Andy can do that too.
Can you?

Andy sees five zebras in the zoo.
What can five zebras do?

They can gallop, clip, clop. . . .
And then they can stop.

Andy can do that too.
Can you?

Andy sees six monkeys in the zoo.
What can six monkeys do?

They can swing in a tree, and sing,
"Chee chee."

Andy can do that too.
Can you?

Andy sees seven little deer in the zoo.
What can seven deer do?

They can jump here and there.
They can leap in the air.

Andy can do that too.
Can you?

Andy sees eight crocodiles in the zoo.
What can eight crocodiles do?

They can wiggle and slide from side to side.

Then Andy sees his friend, Ann, at the ice-cream stand.

What do the two friends do?

They eat ice cream. They count
to ten.

Then Ann hops, skips, jumps through the zoo again. And Andy closes the Word Window.

You can read these ten action words with Andy.

skip

jump

run

gallop

hop

Andy can do that too. Can you?

Andy sees nine little owls in the zoo.
What can nine owls do?

They can flutter and fly when the
moon is high.

Andy can do that too. Can you?

Andy sees ten rabbits in the zoo.
What can ten rabbits do?

They can hop, hop, hop. Then they can
stop. Andy can do that too. Can you?